COUGARS

LIVING WILD

LIVING WILD

Published by Creative Paperbacks
P.O. Box 227, Mankato, Minnesota 56002
Creative Paperbacks is an imprint of The Creative Company
www.thecreativecompany.us

Design and production by Mary Herrmann
Art direction by Rita Marshall
Printed in the United States of America

Photographs by Alamy (BRUCE COLEMAN INC., Corbis Flirt, Danita Delimont, Greg Duncan/Kenebec Images, Val Duncan/Kenebec Images, Buddy Mays, Moviestore collection Ltd, Papilio), Corbis (Marianne Rosenstiehl/Sygma), Dreamstime (Bevanward, Steven Blandin, Wessel Cirkel, Bambi L. Dingman, Jens Klingebiel, Kodo34, Geoffrey Kuchera, Outdoorsman, Warren Price, Seread, Sunheyy), French Ministry of Culture & Communication, Getty Images (Barbara Hesse, Oxford Scientific), iStockphoto (DenGuy, djperry, Images in the Wild, jim kruger, Alexey Stiop, Denis Jr. Tangney, Astrida Valigorsky), NHPA (LAURIE CAMPBELL), Andres Quandelacy, Shutterstock (creativex, jo Crebbin, S. R. Maglione, rook76, worldswildlifewonders)

Library of Congress Cataloging-in-Publication Data
Gish, Melissa.
Cougars / by Melissa Gish.
p. cm. — (Living wild)
Includes bibliographical references and index.
Summary: A look at cougars, including their habitats, physical characteristics such as their tawny coats, behaviors, relationships with humans, and protected status as a game animal in the world today.
ISBN 978-1-60818-167-4 (hardcover)
ISBN 978-0-89812-774-4 (pbk)
1. Puma—Juvenile literature. I. Title.

QL737.C23G5145 2012
599.75'24—dc23   2011035834

First Edition
9 8 7 6 5 4 3 2 1

COUGARS

Melissa Gish

Far from the roads and trails frequented by park visitors, a cougar makes her way

silently along the rocky ledge of a small canyon. She is stalking a mule deer.

It is midsummer in the forests of Yellowstone National Park. Far from the roads and trails frequented by park visitors, a cougar makes her way silently along the rocky ledge of a small canyon. She is stalking a mule deer. Oblivious to the cat's presence, the deer pauses at a bearberry shrub to nibble at the dark green leaves and soft twigs. Suddenly, the cougar leaps off the ledge and lands on the deer's back,

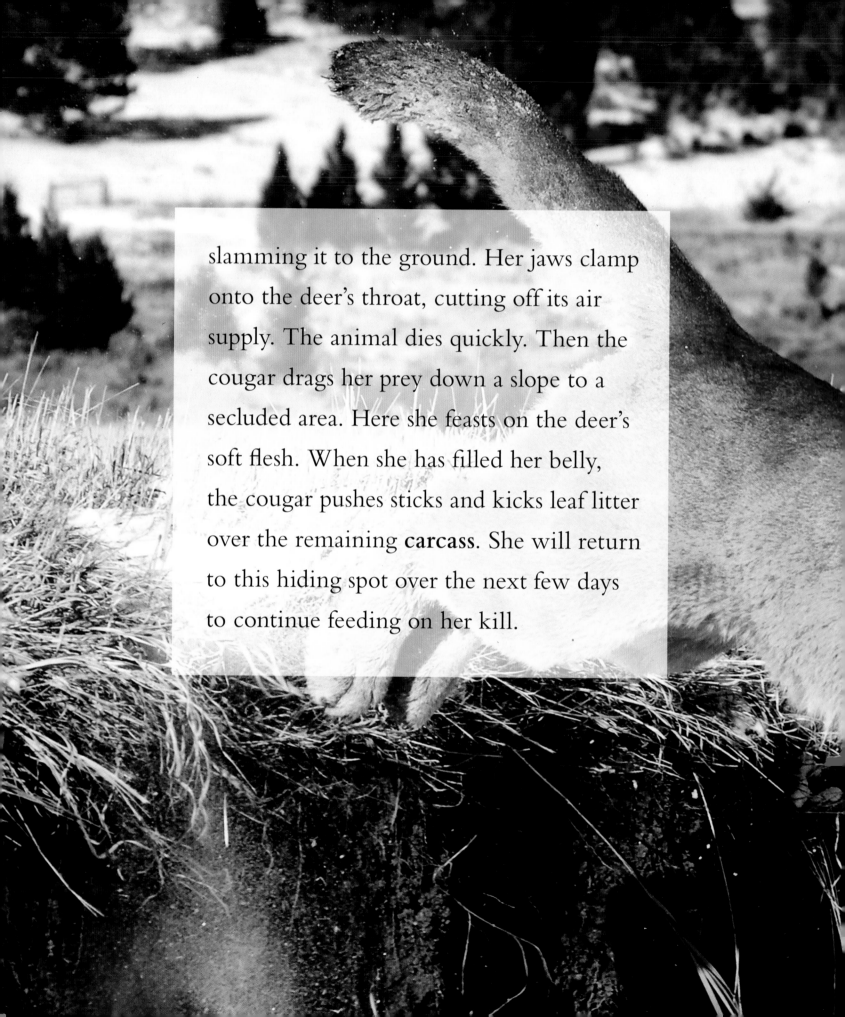

slamming it to the ground. Her jaws clamp onto the deer's throat, cutting off its air supply. The animal dies quickly. Then the cougar drags her prey down a slope to a secluded area. Here she feasts on the deer's soft flesh. When she has filled her belly, the cougar pushes sticks and kicks leaf litter over the remaining **carcass**. She will return to this hiding spot over the next few days to continue feeding on her kill.

WHERE IN THE WORLD THEY LIVE

■ **Argentine Cougar**
Argentina

■ **Costa Rican Cougar**
Costa Rica

■ **Northern South American Cougar**
northern South America

■ **Southern South American Cougar**
southern South America

■ **North American Cougar**
Canada, United States, Mexico

Eastern South American Cougar
Brazil

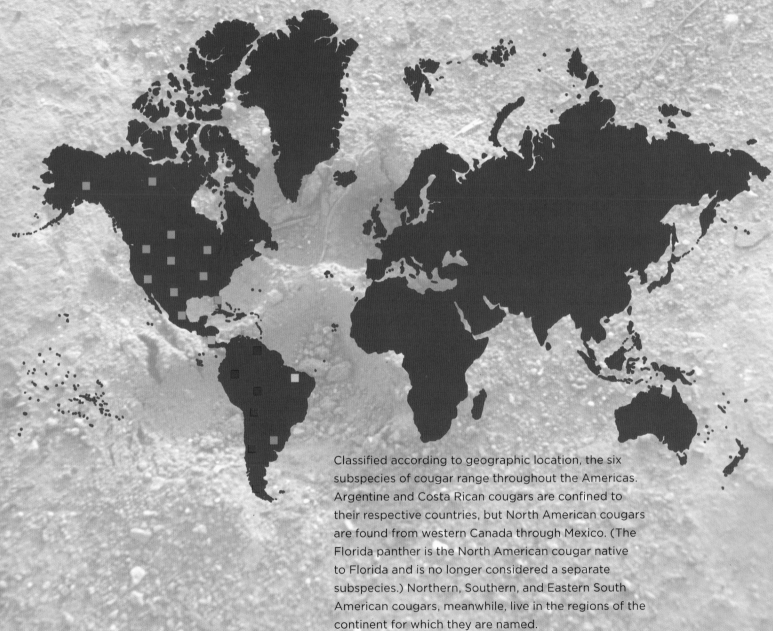

Classified according to geographic location, the six subspecies of cougar range throughout the Americas. Argentine and Costa Rican cougars are confined to their respective countries, but North American cougars are found from western Canada through Mexico. (The Florida panther is the North American cougar native to Florida and is no longer considered a separate subspecies.) Northern, Southern, and Eastern South American cougars, meanwhile, live in the regions of the continent for which they are named.

MOUNTAIN CLIMBING CAT

In its native regions, the jaguarundi is sometimes known as leoncillo, *which is Spanish for "little lion."*

T he cougar is the largest member of the subfamily Felinae, which also encompasses the cheetah of Africa, the ocelot of Central and South America, the lynx of North America, and about 30 other small cats—including **domesticated** cats. Its closest relative is the jaguarundi, which is found from southern Texas to South America and is the only other cat that joins the cougar in the genus *Puma*. Unlike their larger cousins the lions, tigers, and leopards, cougars do not roar. Rather, they vocalize by growling, screeching, and screaming.

The cougar has more nicknames than any other animal in North America. Depending on the region, it is known as a puma, catamount, painter, mountain lion, or panther. The name "panther" is shared with another cougar relative, the jaguar, as well as with the leopard. The cougar's scientific name is *Puma concolor*. The genus name, *Puma*, is a Spanish word that was derived from the name given to these wild cats by the Quechua Indians of Peru. The species name, *concolor*, is Latin for "of one color."

Because they are highly **adaptable**, cougars are the most widespread of all the large predators of the Americas.

While exploring Florida in 1528, Spaniard Álvar Núñez Cabeza de Vaca became the first European in North America to see a cougar.

Despite having color-blindness, or trouble differentiating between certain colors, cougars have excellent vision.

Florida panthers were put on the Endangered Species List in 1967, but conservation efforts have not effectively increased their numbers.

They can survive on rugged mountainsides as far north as Canada's Yukon Territory and as far south as Venezuela's Andes Mountains, as well as in the forests, canyons, and high deserts in between. There are six subspecies of cougar, each defined by its geographical location. The Argentine cougar and the Costa Rican cougar are native to Argentina and Costa Rica respectively. The Northern South American cougar is found across the northern half of South America, from Peru to northern Brazil, while the Southern South American cougar lives in southern parts of the continent. The Eastern South American cougar's range spans from southeastern Brazil to northern Argentina. The North American subspecies has the greatest range of all cougars, from British Columbia to southern Mexico. These cougars are found mostly in the western half of the continent, with scattered populations in the Appalachian Mountains and a small, struggling population in Florida.

Officially named Florida panthers, the cougars in Florida are smaller than cougars found elsewhere in North America and were once considered a separate subspecies. However, recent **DNA** tests revealed that these animals are identical to the cougars inhabiting other regions of North

Florida panthers run the risk of mercury poisoning because high levels of this chemical are present in their prey.

The North American cougar's wide feet and powerful stride enable it to bound through snow with ease.

America. This new information resulted in the Florida panther being removed from the Red List of Threatened Species that is published annually by the International Union for Conservation of Nature (IUCN). Scientists fear that the Florida panther may disappear if protective measures are abandoned. Despite conservation efforts, habitat loss and collisions with vehicles have contributed to the steady decline of these wild cats in Florida.

Cougars are muscular animals with long, powerful legs and broad, rounded feet. Their body size is related to the climate in which they live and their primary food source. Colder temperatures and larger prey equate with heavier cougars. For example, male Florida panthers typically weigh about 130 pounds (59 kg), but cougars in the northwestern United States and Canada average 200 pounds (91 kg). Female cougars are smaller, usually between 75 and 120 pounds (34–54 kg). Cougars stand from 24 to 30 inches (61–76 cm) at the shoulder and can grow to be approximately 6 feet (1.8 m) long. The tail may add an additional two feet (61 cm).

Except for humans, cougars have few natural enemies. These cats typically share their habitats and food sources

Florida panthers are habitat generalists, which means they use a variety of habitats, from swamps to grasslands.

Cougars can adapt as easily to life in deserts at sea level as to life in mountain forests at an elevation of 10,000 feet (3,048 m).

When walking, cougars typically place their hind paw in the previous imprint made by the front paw.

with only two other major predators: brown bears and wolves. Adult brown bears may weigh 1,500 pounds (680 kg), and while wolves typically weigh no more than 80 pounds (36 kg), a cougar is no match for wolves hunting in a pack. When a conflict between a cougar and a competitor occurs, a cougar will almost always run, even if it means abandoning its food. Cougars may end up as prey themselves because they are not strong enough to defend themselves against bears and often cannot outrun a pack of wolves.

Cougars vary in color from tawny to reddish brown. Combined with dark markings on the ears and snout, as well as on the tip of the tail, a cougar's primary fur color provides

camouflage. In desert habitats such as New Mexico and southern Texas, light-colored cougar fur blends in with the surrounding rock, and in forested environments, such as that of Rocky Mountain National Park, dark-colored cougars can virtually disappear in a stand of trees or against a mountainside. Cougars are typically dark on top and light on the underside. This type of camouflage, called countershading, is an asset to cougars, which usually hunt from rocks and ledges above prey. When the light strikes the cougar from the top, it creates a shadow on its lighter underside and makes it less detectable from below.

Cougars are crepuscular animals, which means they are most active during the twilight hours of dawn and

A cougar's eyeshine can be yellow (as shown) or green, perhaps depending on the type of light shone on its eyes.

dusk. With good night vision, cougars are able to see in near darkness. The cougar's eyes are equipped with a reflective layer of tissue called a tapetum lucidum. This tissue collects light and concentrates it in the center of the **retina**, allowing the cougar to see much better than humans can in very low light. The tapetum lucidum causes eyeshine, a condition in which an animal's eyes reflect color when a light source is shined on them. The cougar's eyeshine is often bright yellow, or gold, in color.

Like all cats, cougars have four toes with **retractable** claws to capture and hold prey. They are strict carnivores, meaning they never eat plants. Their powerful jaws and 28 teeth are specialized for eating meat. Four canine teeth are designed to clamp down on prey, and four carnassials, which are situated farther back in the jaw, are used like scissors to shear through flesh and tendons (flexible tissues that attach muscles to bone). To more efficiently devour a meal, cougars also have sharp projections, called papillae, on their tongues that they use like a grater to scrape meat and soft, fatty marrow from bones. Like other cats, cougars do not eat bones. If a cougar should break its canines or carnassials, it would eventually die of starvation.

A cougar's front paws are larger than its hind paws, and each paw has pads under the toes and on the heel.

Cougars are at home in many national parks, including Arizona's Grand Canyon and Utah's Red Cliffs.

CLEVER COUGARS

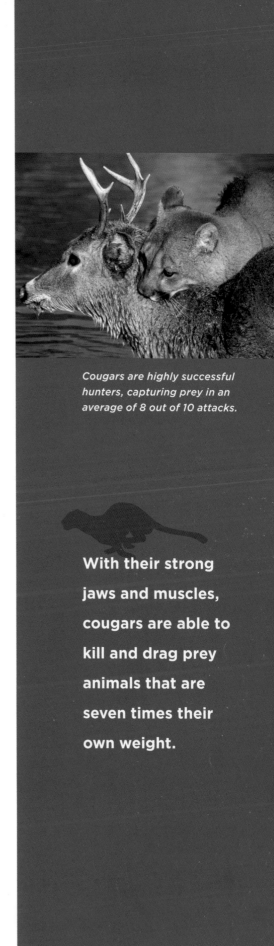

Cougars are highly successful hunters, capturing prey in an average of 8 out of 10 attacks.

With their strong jaws and muscles, cougars are able to kill and drag prey animals that are seven times their own weight.

Hiding in caves, rock crevices, and tall grass, cougars sleep for 12 to 20 hours each day and hunt early in the morning or at night. Cougars regularly hunt a wide range of prey that varies by geographic region. Deer is by far the cougar's favorite meal. Across the U.S., cougars commonly prey on white-tailed deer, and in South America, they stalk pudus and marsh deer.

Although cougars are capable of sprinting at speeds of up to 40 miles (64 km) per hour, they choose to sneak up on prey instead. Thick pads on the bottoms of their feet provide a cushion as they creep silently toward prey. A cougar stalks its prey to within one or two leaps and then launches a high-speed attack to knock it to the ground. While it typically drops down from a high position onto a prey animal's back, a cougar can also cover up to 30 feet (9 m) in a single horizontal leap to capture prey.

Landing full force on a small animal will usually kill it. With larger animals, the cougar will deliver a strong bite to the base of the skull, breaking the prey's neck. Its bite is so strong that a cougar can instantly kill prey as large as a 600-pound (272 kg) moose or bison. Cougars avoid

A cougar may kill two deer per month in cool climates or two deer per week in hot climates—so the meat won't spoil before it's eaten.

landing on the front of an animal, as one kick from a large hoofed animal could break the cougar's back or ribs.

Cougars are considered apex predators, meaning they are at the top of the **food chain**. The cats also contribute to the health of their communities by preying on sick, injured, and old animals. Contrary to common belief, cougars do not stalk and hunt humans. When cougars and humans do cross paths, the outcome can be uncertain, but, in general, cougars prefer to avoid contact with humans as much as possible.

The cougar is a solitary animal, living alone in a particular area called its home range. A male cougar's home range averages 116 square miles (300 sq km), while a female cougar's home range is usually about half that size. A cougar marks the boundaries of its home range by scraping together piles of pine needles, leaf litter, and dirt, and then spraying the piles with urine. A cougar also claws deep gashes in trees and marks them with scent from glands in its face and front foot pads.

Males constantly patrol their territory, marking the boundaries over and over. Females, on the other hand, travel little and scent-mark their boundaries only

occasionally. Cougars may have two home ranges and **migrate** seasonally between them. Higher elevations are home to cougars and their prey in the summer, but when prey animals descend to protected valley forests in the winter, cougars follow them.

Female and male cougars generally stay out of each other's way, except during courtship and mating. Females reach maturity at age two and males at age three or four. Male cougars are drawn to a female that is ready to mate by a certain smell that is released in her urine markings. Females also announce their readiness to mate by making

With a running start, a cougar can leap more than 15 feet (4.5 m) up a tree or onto a rock ledge.

FROM "MOUNTAIN LION"

So, she will never leap up that way again, with the yellow flash of a mountain lion's long shoot!

And her bright striped frost-face will never watch any more, out of the shadow of the cave in the blood-orange rock,

Above the trees of the Lobo dark valley-mouth!

Instead, I look out.

And out to the dim of the desert, like a dream, never real;

To the snow of the Sangre de Cristo Mountains, the ice of the mountains of Picoris,

And near across at the opposite steep of snow, green trees motionless standing in snow, like a Christmas toy.

And I think in this empty world there was room for me and a mountain lion.

And I think in the world beyond, how easily we might spare a million or two humans

And never miss them.

Yet what a gap in the world, the missing white frost-face of that slim yellow mountain lion!

by D. H. Lawrence (1885–1930)

loud vocalizations that sound like human screams. Cougars are polyestrous, meaning they can mate year round. A male and female will come together for about 14 days, hunting and sleeping together in a bonding ritual. They will mate many times to ensure success. Then the male will leave the female and repeat this pattern with several other females throughout the year. Females choose a partner only once every two years.

Before she gives birth, the female cougar selects a secluded den site—a protected place such as a high rock ledge or a cave—where she and her offspring will be safest from predators. The female lines the den with soft plants, leaves, and moss. After 82 to 98 days, the female gives birth to as many as 6 cubs. The cubs weigh only about 14 ounces (397 g) at birth. They have dark spots on their coats and rings on their tails, which gives them camouflage. They have blue eyes that do not open until the cubs are 10 days old. As cubs grow, their eyes will darken to a golden brown, and the spots and rings will disappear.

From the day they are born, cubs communicate with their mother. They mew like domestic kittens, and the mother whistles back at them. Cougars also purr—but

A male cougar licks and bites the back of a female cougar's neck as a way of showing dominance.

Like all cats, cougars lick their legs, shoulders, and hips, covering their fur with wet saliva that **evaporates** to cool their bodies.

When young cougars practice their tree-climbing skills, they sometimes have difficulty getting down again.

they are much louder than domestic cats. The cubs rely on their mother's milk for nourishment for the first three months of their lives, but as soon as six weeks after birth, their mother will introduce them to meat, bringing prey to the den for the cubs to eat.

To teach her young how to hunt, the mother uses her paws to fling pieces of food across the ground, encouraging her cubs to pounce on it. When the cubs are **weaned** at three months of age, they will begin to join their mother on hunts. They learn how to stalk and capture prey by mimicking their mother's movements and practicing on small prey such as mice and rabbits.

By nine months of age, cougar cubs can fend for themselves, yet they remain with their mothers for another 12 to 15 months. It takes time for young cougars to fine-tune their hunting skills, so they continue to hunt with their mother, sharing kills with her, until they are two years old. By this time, the young cougars are fully grown, and their mother will chase them away. The young cougars go off alone in search of territories that have not yet been claimed or that have been abandoned by cougars that have died or moved away. A female may

be allowed to take a portion of her mother's home range and make it her own, but males must move away so they will not be in competition with older males in the area.

It is during this time, when young cougars are roaming widely in search of territory, that they most often come into contact with humans. In the wild, cougars can live 12 to 15 years, but in captivity, cougars may live more than 25 years.

Although cougars prefer to avoid water, adult cougars are stronger and faster swimmers than humans.

The Incas crafted this symbol of the cougar's paw in Sacsayhuamán, a stone complex near Cusco, Peru.

THE SILENT ONE

Masks played a significant role in Incan ceremonies and rituals, and the cougar was an especially important figure.

L ong ago, in South America, the cougar symbolized strength and cunning. Cougar images have appeared on stone carvings and pottery from the times of the Moche people, who existed in ancient Peru from A.D. 100 to 400. In Bolivia, Pumapunku is the site of an ancient temple built in the late sixth century. Its name means "doorway of the cougar" in the language of the Aymara people, a cultural group native to Bolivia, Peru, and Chile. Pumapunku is located at Tiahuanaco, near Lake Titicaca, a lake whose name has sometimes been translated as "Rock of the Puma." To this day, the people of this region revere the cougar as a spiritually important feature of their religion.

Coming to power in the early 15th century, the Inca civilization existed for more than 100 years. The Incas chose to design their capital city, Cusco, in the shape of a cougar. These wild cats were also included in Inca stone carvings, sculptures, and other artwork. Today, Cusco continues to honor the cougar through its art and architecture.

Long before Europeans arrived in the New World, virtually all the **indigenous** tribes of North America, with

Zuni carvers of stone fetishes, or objects believed to hold a certain power, still practice their art today.

the exception of those in the Arctic, accepted cougars as part of their lives. As top predators, cougars were seen as vital contributors to the circle of life. They were hunted for their fur and meat, and they were revered for their powerful connection to the spirit world. In the American Southwest, cougars are still considered spiritual animals by a number of tribes, including the Zuni, Navajo, and Apache.

In many American Indian traditions, the cougar is nicknamed "the silent one." It is seen as a cunning hunter that strikes swiftly and kills quickly, representing leadership and strength. Also, its protective nature in raising offspring is symbolic of motherly devotion and protection. Some tribes, such as the Apache and Hualapai of the American Southwest, consider the cougar to be a messenger to the spirit world and view the screams of a cougar as a sign of impending death.

Today, images of cougars that represent strength and speed are found throughout contemporary culture, particularly in sports. Brigham Young University in Utah, Mount Royal University in Calgary, Columbia College in Missouri, and many other schools proudly feature cougars as their sports teams' mascots. Butch T. Cougar is the mascot of Washington State University in Pullman, Clyde the Cougar represents South Carolina's College of Charleston, and Eddie the Cougar rallies fans at Southern Illinois University in Edwardsville. From 1947 to 1989, the University of Houston's cougar mascot was a live cat. Five different captive cougars filled the role of Shasta over the years until the college decided to switch to a costumed cougar in 1989.

Early in America's history, cougars thrived in the eastern states. There they were called panthers. For this reason, the National Football League (NFL) team from Charlotte, North Carolina, became the Carolina Panthers, and the National Hockey League (NHL) team from Sunrise, Florida, became the Florida Panthers. Both teams' logos feature the characteristic long whiskers and toothy snarl of an attacking cougar. Even an athletic shoe company—Puma—chose the well-known wild cat for its name and features a leaping cougar as its logo.

For more than three decades, from 1967 to 2002, Ford Motor Company's Mercury Cougar was a cornerstone of the car manufacturer's empire. Introduced as a "muscle car," a sporty vehicle with a powerful engine, the Cougar

Washington State University adopted the cougar as its mascot in 1919, changing the logo over the years.

Scientists believe that cougars are more closely related to African cheetahs than to their neighboring relatives, jaguars and ocelots.

gave rise to Mercury's logo: the "sign of the cat," which featured a snarling cougar atop a Ford/Mercury sign. This symbol projected an image of the company's leadership in the U.S. sports car industry.

A less fearsome image of the cougar was presented in 1959, when the American animation studio Hanna-Barbera introduced Snagglepuss, a cougar who wore a bowtie. Snagglepuss was orange in his first cartoon, *Lamb Chopped* (featured on the *Quick Draw McGraw Show*), but was colored pink for the remainder of his career, which included appearances in Kellogg's Cocoa Krispies commercials in the 1960s. Snagglepuss hasn't appeared regularly on television since the late 1970s, but he can occasionally be seen on the *Yogi Bear Show* and the *Quick Draw McGraw Show*, which are **syndicated** on several U.S. and Canadian television networks.

Perhaps better known than Snagglepuss is the Pink Panther, who first appeared in 1964. The silent cougar with a sense of humor and a sneaky streak starred in more than 120 cartoons, 10 television shows, and 3 TV specials. One of his most recent shows, *Pink Panther and Pals*, was part of the Cartoon Network's lineup in 2009. While the Pink Panther

Because he never spoke, the Pink Panther had to express himself with body language in cartoons.

never showed his teeth or snarled at anyone, he did exhibit the patience and cleverness characteristic of real cougars.

He may not be a real cougar, but Thomas Fireheart— better known to fans of the Spider-Man universe as the superhuman character named Puma—knows all about the strength and speed of these amazing cats. First introduced as a villain in the comic *Amazing Spider-Man* in 1984, Puma later appeared as a Spider-Man ally. With razor-sharp fangs and claws, Puma has lent his agile fighting skills to the *Avengers*, *X-Men*, and *Marvel Divas* series as well.

Less intimidating cougars are featured in Jane Gilley's children's story *The Phantom Puma* (2008) and Patti

The 1977 Canadian 12-cent stamp depicted the cougar poised in a typical hunting position, ready to pounce.

An average adult cougar must eat 8 to 10 pounds (3.6–4.5 kg) of meat—about 6 percent of its body weight—each day to remain healthy.

Suits's tale for young readers, *Topa and the Path of the Puma* (2008), about two boys living in cougar country in the Andes Mountains. Jean Craighead George's classic 1960s series Thirteen Moons, which was recently reissued under the name Seasons of the Moon (2001–02), includes a story about a male cougar who "adopts" two orphaned cougar cubs, and C. W. Anderson's series of Billy and Blaze adventure books (featuring a boy and his horse) includes the reissued 1993 book *Blaze and the Mountain Lion.*

Encounters with cougars are not limited to fictional stories, though. Because people in the western U.S. may cross paths with real cougars, many books about the relationships between humans and cougars have been published in recent years. David Baron's *The Beast in the Garden* (2003) examines what happens when suburban areas are woven into the fabric of existing cougar populations. Green spaces that welcome deer and small **mammals** in order to provide neighborhoods with a natural setting inevitably draw predators such as cougars as well—which can have unfortunate results, if cougars attack not only the deer but also pets in people's backyards.

People in protected wilderness areas may encounter cougars in unexpected locations, such as atop roofs.

CLOSE ENCOUNTERS OF A COUGAR KIND

France's Chauvet Cave, near the Pont-d'Arc (above), contains the oldest known cave paintings, some of which depict 30,000-year-old cougar ancestors (opposite).

T he first true cats, or felids, **evolved** about 25 million years ago and migrated all over the world. About 20 million years ago, a group of felid ancestors called *Pseudaelurus* emerged in Europe and Asia. These creatures evolved over the next 12 million years, with some species traveling to North America across the Bering **Land Bridge**. At first, they were about the same size as modern cougars. As they slowly made their way south into Central and South America to escape the effects of the ice age that was spreading across North America, they became agile climbers in the dense tropical jungles.

About 8,000 years ago, as the glaciers, or huge sheets of ice, covering North America were receding and the climate was warming once again, some cougars migrated northward. Changing little as they spread across their vast habitat, these species gave rise to the cougars we know today. Other prehistoric felids remained in their tropical habitats, evolving into eight subspecies of jaguarundi and more distant cougar relatives such as the jaguar, ocelot, and margay.

Although cougars were respected by indigenous peoples and allowed to flourish for hundreds of years, this began

Some rules to follow in cougar country are: carry a walking stick, keep children close, and walk rather than jog.

Park rangers advise people who encounter cougars to wave their arms to look bigger and to never run away, which invites a chase.

to change in the 16th century. Immediately seen by European explorers and settlers as competitors for game and threats to domestic livestock, cougars were targeted for destruction. Bounty hunting of cougars began in the 1500s, when Jesuit priests in Southern California offered American Indians a bounty, or reward, of one bull for each cougar killed. Later, many eastern states, including Connecticut, Pennsylvania, and Massachusetts, enacted cougar bounty hunting as well. By the mid-1800s, the cougar had been wiped out of most of the eastern two-thirds of the U.S. Only scattered populations survived, with reported sightings in Maine, Virginia, West Virginia, Georgia, and Florida. Fifty years later, even these cougars were completely gone except for a small population that remained hidden in the swamps of southern Florida.

Because the American West was still relatively unpopulated by white settlers in the 1800s, cougars were able to thrive in the rugged environment. However, as settlers moved westward, the cougar seemed to be in their way. The West's major move against cougars began in 1888, with Utah's classification of cougars as "obnoxious animals." Many states—including Washington, California,

Colorado, Idaho, and New Mexico—as well as Canada's British Columbia followed suit and enacted bounties. As a result, cougar hunting intensified, and the cats were in danger of becoming systematically eradicated from North America.

A movement toward environmentalism and conservation in the mid-20th century prompted people to take a second look at the cougar. The cat's status was legally changed from predatory animal to game animal, which meant cougar hunters now needed a permit and would be restricted on the number they could kill. Slowly, the populations of cougars in the West began to

Young animals unfamiliar with a cougar's territorial manner may find themselves in trouble on a cougar trail.

Cougars fearlessly attack porcupines, causing some people to believe that the cats are to blame for porcupines' decline in Texas.

increase. Current numbers vary by state, with California and Texas having the largest populations (about 6,000 each), followed by other states such as Oregon (with 5,000) and Arizona (with 3,000). Scientists estimate that only 100 to 160 cougars exist in the entire state of Florida, and a handful of cougars are believed to remain in scattered areas of the Appalachian Mountains.

At first, efforts to save the cougar seemed to be worthwhile, but after 1990, when California became the only state to legally protect the species, debate sprang up concerning the wild cat's protection status in other states. A hunting ban, critics argued, would have serious effects on prey animals in cougar habitats. Such debate has continued, particularly in Texas, where ranchers are concerned that the increase in cougars has led to a decline in the populations of deer, elk, porcupines, and other popular cougar prey, resulting in the cougars' turning to domestic livestock for their meals. Ranchers have called for an increase in cougar hunting permits.

In heavily populated states such as California and Washington, understanding the effects of human encounters with cougars is typically the focal point of cougar research. Since 1890, North American cougars have fatally attacked humans only about 20 times. Pet dogs are responsible for 10 to 20 human deaths each year, and bees kill an average of 53 people per year. The chances of being attacked by a cougar are comparatively slim, yet human-cougar interactions are on the rise.

To learn about cougar migration and hunting habits near urban areas, researchers capture, tag, and track cougars. Like many wildlife management agencies in the West, the Arizona Game and Fish Department conducts studies of cougars. The researchers tranquilize a cougar to make it fall asleep. Then a **radio collar** is placed around the cat's neck. Such collars weigh about two pounds (0.9 kg), are made of several layers of heavy-duty belt material, have two small antennae on top, an aluminum compartment for the battery—which can last up to two years—and the **Global Positioning System** (GPS) tracking device on the bottom. The GPS transmitter sends data on the animal's movements to **satellites**, allowing researchers to monitor the cougar in the wild.

The data is used to help wildlife managers and conservationists create strategies for balancing the needs of

A tranquilized cougar's eyes remain open while the cat is asleep and may need to be moistened by researchers.

As expert tree climbers, cougars can jump 8 to 15 feet (2.4–4.6 m) straight up, climb quickly, and safely drop 65 feet (19.8 m).

cougars and humans. In rural areas of New Mexico, Colorado, and Texas, where cattle ranchers privately own much of the land, these ranchers hunt—and sell permits to hunt—on their land. In many portions of the Southwest, the overhunting of deer, elk, peccaries, and other types of cougar prey has led to a decline of these species, forcing cougars to take after larger, yet more easily available, food sources—namely, cattle. Research on cougar behaviors may help ranchers and cougars live in peace instead of in competition.

Cougars also come into contact with humans in urban areas. **Deforestation** caused by urban development, logging, mining, or agriculture breaks cougar habitats into small sections, forcing cougars into populated areas to search for food. While cougars prefer to avoid humans, a starving cougar makes no distinction between a mule deer and a bicyclist on a park trail. Tragedy has resulted from cougar-human interaction, but as a large predator, the cougar is vital to the health of its mountain community. Researchers have only begun to uncover the mysteries of the cougar, an amazing cat with more secrets to reveal—if only we can learn to survive together.

Young cougars mimic their mother's behavior in every way, learning new skills and strengthening their muscles.

ANIMAL TALE: WHY COUGAR IS LONG AND SLENDER

The cougar is a strong, sleek hunter. This American Indian tale from the Blackfeet tribe of the northwestern U.S. explains how the cougar got its slender body and long tail.

A long time ago, the cougar was short and round like Badger. He had a short, fluffy tail and silky fur. Cougar rarely hunted, choosing instead to steal others' food.

The one who made all the birds and animals of the world was called Old Man. One day, when Old Man was walking through the forest, he saw some squirrels playing tag around a fire. Old Man watched from behind a tree as the mob of squirrels caught the one who was "it" and quickly knocked him to the ground. They threw hot ashes over him, but the moment the buried squirrel cried out, the others uncovered him. Then the squirrels picked another squirrel to be "it," chasing and burying him in this way.

This foolish game went on for some time. As Old Man watched, he started to get hungry. Then he got an idea. Stepping out from behind the tree, Old Man asked, "May I play with you?"

At first, the squirrels were afraid, but soon they were chasing Old Man around the fire. When they caught him, they tackled him and covered him with hot ashes. When Old Man cried out, the squirrels uncovered him. Then Old Man chased the squirrels. But instead of catching just one, he caught all the squirrels and buried them in hot ashes. And when they cried out, he threw more hot ashes on them.

Soon the squirrels were cooked quite nicely, and Old Man began to feast on them. He had eaten only half of the squirrels when he grew

sleepy and curled up on the ground for a nap.

Just about this time, Cougar happened by. Spying the lovely roasted squirrels, Cougar could not resist stealing from Old Man. After he ate all the squirrels, Cougar hurried away to hide from Old Man, whom he knew would surely be angry.

When Old Man woke up and discovered that he had been robbed, he was indeed furious. He followed Cougar's tracks through the forest until he found Cougar sleeping on a rock high on a ledge. Old Man put his boot down on the back of Cougar's neck and grabbed Cougar's tail in his hands.

"What are you doing?" Cougar cried out.

"You stole my squirrel supper!" raged Old Man. "I think it's time to teach you a lesson." And with that, he began pulling Cougar's tail while holding his boot against Cougar's neck.

Cougar yowled as his body stretched like a bowstring. Old Man nearly ripped Cougar in half. Then Old Man took Cougar's tail in both hands and swung the cat around and around. Cougar's tail stretched longer and longer until it was nearly the length of Cougar's long body. Then Old Man held the tip of Cougar's tail to the fire, singeing it black. He rubbed hot ashes on cougar's head, making black marks on Cougar's muzzle and ears.

"Now you are not so smart, are you?" said Old Man. "No more are you a fat and lazy thief. You will have to work for your food like everyone else."

And Cougar does. Long and slender, always hungry, Cougar constantly prowls for a meal.

GLOSSARY

adaptable – having the ability to change to improve one's chances of survival in an environment

camouflage – the ability to hide, due to coloring or markings that blend in with a given environment

carcass – the dead body of an animal

deforestation – the clearing away of trees from a forest

DNA – deoxyribonucleic acid; a substance found in every living thing that determines the species and individual characteristics of that thing

domesticated – tamed to be kept as a pet or used as a work animal

evaporates – changes from liquid to invisible vapor or gas

evolved – gradually developed into a new form

food chain – a system in nature in which living things are dependent on each other for food

Global Positioning System – a system of satellites, computers, and other electronic devices that work together to determine the location of objects or living things that carry a trackable device

indigenous – originating in a particular region or country

land bridge – a piece of land connecting two landmasses that allowed people and animals to pass from one place to another

mammals – warm-blooded animals that have a backbone and hair or fur, give birth to live young, and produce milk to feed their young

migrate – to undertake a regular, seasonal journey from one place to another and then back again

parasitic – being an animal or plant that lives on or inside another living thing (called a host) while giving nothing back to the host; some parasitic organisms cause disease or even death

radio collar – a collar fitted with a small electronic device that sends a signal to a radio receiver

retina – a layer or lining in the back of the eye that is sensitive to light

retractable – able to be drawn in from an extended position

satellites – mechanical devices launched into space; they may be designed to travel around Earth or toward other planets or the sun

syndicated – broadcast to many television stations at the same time

weaned – made the young of a mammal accept food other than nursing milk

SELECTED BIBLIOGRAPHY

Bekoff, Marc, and Cara Blessley Lowe, eds. *Listening to Cougar.* Boulder: University Press of Colorado, 2008.

Bolgiano, Chris, and Jerry Roberts, eds. *The Eastern Cougar: Historic Accounts, Scientific Investigations, and New Evidence.* Mechanicsburg, Pa.: Stackpole Books, 2005.

Deurbrouck, Jo. *Stalked by a Mountain Lion: Fear, Fact, and the Uncertain Future of Cougars in America.* Kingwood, Tex.: Falcon Publishing, 2007.

Hornocker, Maurice, and Sharon Negri, eds. *Cougar: Ecology and Conservation.* Chicago: University of Chicago Press, 2009.

National Geographic. "Animals: Mountain Lion." http://animals.nationalgeographic.com/animals/mammals/mountain-lion/.

San Diego Zoo. "Animal Bytes: Mountain Lion (Puma, Cougar)." http://www.sandiegozoo.org/animalbytes/t-puma.html.